George Washington Carver

Published in the United States of America by Cherry Lake Publishing
Ann Arbor, Michigan
www.cherrylakepublishing.com

Content Adviser: Jessica Criales, Doctoral Candidate, History Department, Rutgers University
Reading Adviser: Marla Conn MS, Ed., Literacy specialist, Read-Ability, Inc.
Book Design: Jennifer Wahi
Illustrator: Jeff Bane

Photo Credits: ©Matt Wunder/Shutterstock, 5; ©Monkey Business Images/Shutterstock, 7; ©Fotokostic/ Shutterstock, 9; ©PD-US Frances Benjamin Johnston, 11, 22; ©Ben Trahair/Shutterstock, 13; ©nednapa/ Shutterstock, 15; ©iravgustin/Shutterstock, 17; ©PD-US Arthur Rothstein, 19, 23; ©PD-US NYPL Digital Collections, 21; Cover, 8, 12, 16, Jeff Bane; Various frames throughout, ©Shutterstock Images

Library of Congress Cataloging-in-Publication Data

Names: Marsico, Katie, 1980- author. | Bane, Jeff, 1957- illustrator.
Title: George Washington Carver / by Katie Marsico ; [illustrator, Jeff Bane].
Description: Ann Arbor : Cherry Lake Publishing, c2018. | Series: My
   itty-bitty bio | Includes bibliographical references and index.
Identifiers: LCCN 2018003105| ISBN 9781534128781 (hardcover) | ISBN
   9781534130487 (pdf) | ISBN 9781534131989 (pbk.) | ISBN 9781534133686
   (hosted ebook)
Subjects: LCSH: Carver, George Washington, 1864?-1943--Juvenile literature. |
   Agriculturists--United States--Juvenile literature. | African American
   agriculturists--Biography--Juvenile literature.
Classification: LCC S417.C3 M293 2018 | DDC 630.92 [B] --dc23
LC record available at https://lccn.loc.gov/2018003105

Printed in the United States of America
Corporate Graphics

About the author: Katie Marsico is the author of more than 200 reference books for children and young adults. She lives with her husband and six children near Chicago, Illinois.

About the illustrator: Jeff Bane and his two business partners own a studio along the American River in Folsom, California, home of the 1849 Gold Rush. When Jeff's not sketching or illustrating for clients, he's either swimming or kayaking in the river to relax.

I was born on a farm in Missouri.
It belonged to the Carver family.

My parents were **slaves**.
The Carvers owned my mother.

My father died before I was born.

Slave traders **kidnapped** my mother. I was just a baby.

After that, the Carvers raised me.

I went to college in Iowa.

I studied **agriculture**.

I became a **scientist**. I taught at a college for black students.

I helped them learn to be better farmers.

How do you want to help people?

Farmers in the South planted cotton for years. It wore out the **soil**.

I told farmers to try different **crops**. I suggested peanuts.

Planting peanuts made the soil better.

Farmers grew more peanuts than they could sell.

What type of crop would you grow?

I found more than 300 uses for peanuts.

Some involved soap, paint, and glue!

Both whites and blacks respected me.

I gave talks. I said whites and blacks should have equal rights.

Why is it important to be respected?

I died in 1943. My ideas changed lives.

They helped farmers. They made people think about **equality**.

What would you like to ask me?

1896

1860

Born
1865

22

1920

1960

Died
1943

glossary

agriculture (AG-gri-kuhl-chuhr) the raising of crops and animals

crops (KRAHPS) plants grown for food for people or animals

equality (ih-KWAH-lih-tee) the right of everyone to be treated the same

kidnapped (KID-napd) to take and keep someone illegally

scientist (SYE-un-tist) someone who studies nature and the world we live in

slaves (SLAYVZ) people who are owned by other people

soil (SOYL) the top layer of dirt where plants grow

index